VIRTUAL FIELD TRIPS

MARTIN LUTHER KING, JR.
NATIONAL HISTORIC SITE

A MyReportLinks.com Book

Wim Coleman and Pat Perrin

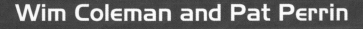
MyReportLinks.com Books
an imprint of

Enslow Publishers, Inc.
Box 398, 40 Industrial Road
Berkeley Heights, NJ 07922
USA

MyReportLinks.com Books, an imprint of Enslow Publishers, Inc. MyReportLinks®
is a registered trademark of Enslow Publishers, Inc.

Library of Congress Cataloging-in-Publication Data

Coleman, Wim.
  Martin Luther King, Jr., National Historic Site / Wim Coleman & Pat Perrin.
    p. cm.
  Includes bibliographical references and index.
  ISBN 0-7660-5225-7
  1. Martin Luther King, Jr., National Historic Site (Atlanta, Ga.)—Juvenile literature. 2. Atlanta (Ga.)—
Buildings, structures, etc.—Juvenile literature. 3. King, Martin Luther, Jr., 1929-1968—Juvenile literature.
4. African American civil rights workers—Biography—Juvenile literature. I. Perrin, Pat. II. Title.
  F294.A88M3733 2005
  323'.092—dc22

                              2004009002

Printed in the United States of America

10 9 8 7 6 5 4 3 2 1

To Our Readers:
Through the purchase of this book, you and your library gain access to the Report Links that specifically back
up this book.
The Publisher will provide access to the Report Links that back up this book and will keep these Report Links
up to date on **www.myreportlinks.com** for five years from the book's first publication date.
We have done our best to make sure all Internet addresses in this book were active and appropriate when we
went to press. However, the author and the Publisher have no control over, and assume no liability for, the
material available on those Internet sites or on other Web sites they may link to.
The usage of the MyReportLinks.com Books Web site is subject to the terms and conditions stated on the
Usage Policy Statement on **www.myreportlinks.com**.
A password may be required to access the Report Links that back up this book. The password is found on the
bottom of page 4 of this book.
Any comments or suggestions can be sent by e-mail to comments@myreportlinks.com or to the address on
the back cover.

Cover Description: On top, is an image of Dr. King at the podium giving his "I Have A Dream" speech. At
left, is King waving to the crowd before the speech. In the background, is his birth home.

MyReportLinks.com Books
Great Books, Great Links, Great for Research!

The Internet sites listed on the next four pages can save you hours of research time. These Internet sites—we call them "Report Links"—are constantly changing, but we keep them up to date on our Web site.

Give it a try! Type http://www.myreportlinks.com into your browser, click on the series title, then the book title, and scroll down to the Report Links listed for this book.

The Report Links will bring you to great source documents, photographs, and illustrations. MyReportLinks.com Books save you time, feature Report Links that are kept up to date, and make report writing easier than ever!

Please see "To Our Readers" on the copyright page for important information about this book, the MyReportLinks.com Web site, and the Report Links that back up this book.

Please enter **FTM1673** if asked for a password.

The Internet sites described below can be accessed at
http://www.myreportlinks.com

*EDITOR'S CHOICE

▶**Martin Luther King, Jr., National Historic Site**
The Martin Luther King, Jr., National Historic Site covers thirty-nine acres. It includes the Ebenezer Baptist Church, the King Center, Peace Plaza, Fire Station No. 6, and his birth home.

*EDITOR'S CHOICE

▶**The King Center**
Founded by Coretta Scott King in 1968, the King Center stands as a tribute to her husband's life. Its mission is to advance Martin Luther King, Jr.'s, legacy of nonviolence, justice, peace, and freedom.

*EDITOR'S CHOICE

▶**We Shall Overcome: Lincoln Memorial**
On August 28, 1963, over two hundred thousand people gathered at the Lincoln Memorial and listened to Martin Luther King, Jr., recite his most famous speech. Read an excerpt from "I Have a Dream" at this Web site.

*EDITOR'S CHOICE

▶**The Martin Luther King, Jr., Papers Project**
The preservation and publication of Dr. King's significant correspondence, sermons, speeches, published writings, and unpublished manuscripts is the focus of this project.

*EDITOR'S CHOICE

▶**Martin Luther King**
Martin Luther King had a dream that all races would live together in racial harmony with equality for all. Learn more about segregation and how King helped change America forever.

*EDITOR'S CHOICE

▶**The Martin Luther King We Remember**
Martin Luther King fought for change against great adversity. He was courageous and a hero. He was also a person who made mistakes. Learn more about his life and times.

Report Links

The Internet sites described below can be accessed at http://www.myreportlinks.com

▶**Center for Voting and Democracy**

The Center for Voting and Democracy is a nonprofit organization that represents all voters and is dedicated to fair elections. The center conducts research and is an advocate for more democratic voting systems.

▶**Civil Rights Act of 1964**

The Civil Rights Act of 1964 is considered the most important United States law on civil rights since the Reconstruction era. This legislation made it illegal to discriminate based on race, color, religion, or national origin.

▶**The Civil Rights Era**

The song "We Shall Overcome" became the anthem for those challenging the government and society to abolish segregation and discrimination. Read about the African-American struggle for racial equality.

▶**The Civil Rights Movement and the Legacy of Martin Luther King, Jr.**

Martin Luther King, Jr., led the civil rights movement in the United States. He was not the first nor the last to fight for freedom and equality. Learn more about people like Malcolm X and Jesse Jackson.

▶**Civil Rights Time Line**

The fight for equality and civil rights in the United States was particularly active in the years spanning 1954 through 1971. Read about some of the more important events in this summarized time line.

▶**"I Have a Dream" by Martin Luther King, Jr., August 28, 1963**

Delivered on the steps of the Lincoln Memorial in Washington, D.C., Martin Luther King, Jr.'s, "I Have a Dream" speech is credited with mobilizing supporters of desegregation and prompting the 1964 Civil Rights Act.

▶**James Earl Ray Fired One Shot at Dr. Martin Luther King, Jr., the Shot Killed Dr. King**

James Earl Ray was convicted of assassinating Martin Luther King, Jr., in Memphis, Tennessee, on April 4, 1968. Detailed investigative information and testimony is presented on the case in this report.

▶**Letter from a Birmingham Jail**

On Good Friday 1963, Rev. Martin Luther King, Jr., and fifty-two others protested segregation by marching in downtown Birmingham, Alabama. They were arrested. King's "Letter From Birmingham Jail" resulted in a turning point in the civil rights movement. Read the letter.

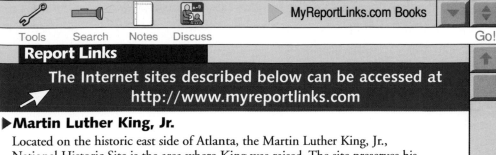

The Internet sites described below can be accessed at http://www.myreportlinks.com

▶**Martin Luther King, Jr.**

Located on the historic east side of Atlanta, the Martin Luther King, Jr., National Historic Site is the area where King was raised. The site preserves his boyhood home and the larger neighborhood called "Sweet Auburn," where he grew up.

▶**Martin Luther King, Jr.: Freedom of Information Act**

Available in two parts, Martin Luther King, Jr.'s, FBI files are now available through the Freedom of Information Act. The files are in PDF format.

▶**Martin Luther King, Jr.: Girl Power**

Written for young people, this overview of Martin Luther King, Jr., and his life describes a concept that was a big part of his philosophy: nonviolence. Read more about it.

▶**Martin Luther King, Jr., Tribute**

View photographs of Martin Luther King, Jr., that appeared in *Life* magazine. In some, he is pictured with his family. In others, we see him at demonstrations.

▶**Martin Luther King, Jr., African-American Civil Rights Leader**

Martin Luther King, Jr., gave a speech on the steps of the Lincoln Memorial. The day was August 28, 1963, and his "I Have a Dream" speech moved the nation. Click on the sound file to hear the entire speech.

▶**MLK Day of Service**

The King Day of Service is a time to solve social problems through community service. Learn how you can continue Martin Luther King, Jr.'s, legacy at this Web site.

▶**National Civil Rights Museum**

The National Civil Rights Museum is located in Memphis, Tennessee, on the site of the old Lorraine Motel, where Martin Luther King, Jr., was assassinated. Exhibits include information on Jim Crow laws and student sit-ins.

▶**The Nobel Peace Prize 1964**

In 1964, Martin Luther King became the youngest person to receive the Nobel Peace Prize. Read his Nobel lecture, "The Quest for Peace and Justice."

Report Links

▶**Robert F. Kennedy: On the Death of Martin Luther King, 1968**

Shortly after the assassination of Martin Luther King, Robert F. Kennedy spoke of the civil rights leader. He asked that America face the horrible news as King himself would have wanted—in a nonviolent way. You can read Kennedy's speech at this Web site.

▶**Rosa and Raymond Parks Institute for Self Development**

Rosa Parks is considered the mother of the civil rights movement. Her organization works to motivate young people to be their best, and to promote multicultural cooperation. Learn more.

▶**Rosa Parks**

Rosa Parks is known as the mother of the civil rights movement. Read more about this brave woman at this Web site.

▶**Spotlight on Mrs. Rosa Parks, Mother of the Civil Rights Movement**

When Rosa Parks refused to give up her seat on a city bus for a white person, the civil rights movement gathered momentum and attention. Learn how Rosa Parks helped to change the world.

▶**Sweet Auburn Historic District: Atlanta**

Sweet Auburn, an African-American neighborhood in Atlanta, Georgia, was a successful and stable community during the time of segregation. Links to King's biography and a photograph of his boyhood home in the neighborhood are available on this Web site.

▶**Today in History: January 15**

Read a summarized biography of Martin Luther King, Jr.'s, life. You can also read his speeches and link to other interesting sites about the African-American experience.

▶**The Voting Rights Act Of 1965**

Until 1965, poll taxes, literacy tests, harassment, and physical violence kept African Americans in the South from voting. This changed with the Voting Rights Act of 1965, passed after years of marches and demonstrations demanding an equal right to vote.

▶**We Shall Overcome: Historic Places of the Civil Rights Movement**

This Web site documents important sites associated with the civil rights movement, including Malcolm X's home in Omaha, Nebraska, and Woolworth's Five & Dime in Greensboro, North Carolina, the site of important student sit-ins.

The Martin Luther King, Jr., National Historic Site is located in Atlanta, Georgia, 1.25 miles east of the central business district.

The park contains about 39 acres, 4.78 of which are owned by the federal government.

The U.S. National Park Service established the Martin Luther King, Jr., National Historic Site in 1980. Its purpose is to protect and interpret the places where Dr. King was born, worked, worshiped, and is buried.

Martin Luther King, Jr., was born in Atlanta on January 15, 1929. He became the outstanding leader of America's civil rights movement.

The civil rights movement was at its height from about 1955 until 1965. It was a protest against the restrictions that some states placed on the rights of African-American citizens.

In 1964, Congress passed the Civil Rights Act and in 1965, the Voting Rights Act, guaranteeing basic civil rights for all Americans, regardless of race.

Martin Luther King, Jr., was assassinated on April 4, 1968, in Memphis, Tennessee.

James Earl Ray pleaded guilty to killing Dr. King. Yet, many believe that Ray did not act alone. The King family believes that Ray was innocent. Ray attempted to get a new trial before he died in prison in 1998.

In 1983, President Ronald Reagan signed legislation creating the Martin Luther King, Jr., National Holiday. It is celebrated on the third Monday of every January.

The King Center was founded in 1968 by Coretta Scott King. Its main goal is to develop and spread programs to educate the world about Dr. King's teachings.

Chapter 1

"Please Be Peaceful"

"Your house has been bombed," Reverend Ralph Abernathy told the young Baptist minister.[1] Martin Luther King, Jr., asked if his wife and baby were all right. Abernathy replied that someone was checking on them.

King and Abernathy were both African American. They were attending a meeting in Montgomery, Alabama. Abernathy was pastor of the First Baptist Church, where the meeting was being held. King was the pastor of Montgomery's Dexter Avenue Baptist Church.

King urged the others at the meeting not to panic. He asked them to go straight home peacefully. King was then driven home where he found hundreds of people gathered in front of his house. Policemen were trying to clear the streets, but the crowd mostly ignored their efforts.[2]

The bomb had gone off on the front porch, destroying part of the house. King rushed inside. He found that his wife, Coretta, and daughter, Yoki (Yolanda), were all right. They were not injured, and Coretta appeared calm. King said that Coretta's self-control helped to calm him down, too.[3]

His family was safe. Now, Martin Luther King had to prevent violence from breaking out in his own front yard.

▶ The Montgomery Bus Boycott

The bombing took place on the night of January 30, 1956. Much of Montgomery, Alabama, was already in an uproar when it happened.

Just two months earlier, on December 1, 1955, an African-American seamstress had been riding a city bus home from work.

▲ *Martin Luther King, Jr., sits in at one of his many press conferences. The reverend became known around the world as the leader of the civil rights movement after his involvement in the Montgomery bus boycott.*

When the bus began to fill up, the driver ordered the seamstress to give up her seat to a white man. The woman—whose name was Rosa Parks—refused to move. She was arrested and taken to jail.

The Montgomery African-American community held meetings to decide what to do. How should they respond to Rosa Parks's arrest? They decided to boycott the bus company.

To coordinate their efforts, in 1955 the community formed the Montgomery Improvement Association (MIA). Martin Luther King became the first president of the MIA, and Ralph David Abernathy became its program director.

Rosa and Raymond Parks Institute for Self Development - Microsoft Internet Explorer

File   Edit   View   Favorites   Tools   Help

Address   http://www.rosaparks.org/

We encourage youth
to reach their highest potential
through the Rosa Parks philosophy
of "Quiet Strength."

Quiet Strength incorporates life skills
which demonstrate dignity with pride,
courage with perseverance
and power with discipline
in a comfortable environment of peace.

ROSA & RAYMOND
PARKS
INSTITUTE FOR SELF DEVELOPMENT

Help Celebrate Mrs. Parks' 91st Birthday!

Background/History   Overview   Programs   Education   Sponsorship   Donations

Pathways To Freedom

General Information: (313) 965-0606   General E-Mail: general@rosaparks.org

Site by Brainwrap Web Design

104779

the ROSA PARKS story
starring Angela Bassett
Available on VHS & DVD

▲ On December 1, 1955, Rosa Parks was arrested for refusing to give up her seat
to a white man on a bus in Montgomery, Alabama. In 1987, Parks co-founded
the Rosa & Raymond Parks Institute for Self Development to help continue the
fight for equal rights.

King's home was bombed during the bus boycott. The protest continued for 381 days until November 1956. Then the United States Supreme Court declared that racially separated seating on public transportation was unconstitutional.

▶ The Situation in the South

In 1868, the Fourteenth Amendment was added to the United States Constitution. This amendment is so important that its key section should be remembered: "No State shall abridge the privileges or immunities of citizens of the United States, nor shall any State deprive any person of life, liberty, or property without due process of law, nor deny any person within its jurisdiction the equal protection of the laws."

Then in 1870, the Fifteenth Amendment was added to the United States Constitution. This made it illegal for any state to deny anyone, including African Americans, the right to vote "on account of race, color, or previous condition of servitude." However, Southern governments used poll taxes and literacy tests to keep African-American citizens from voting. After ninety-five years of tolerating state interference with the voting rights of African Americans, Congress passed the Voting Rights Act of 1965. This act required Southern states to follow specific rules to protect the rights of African Americans who wished to vote for public officials.

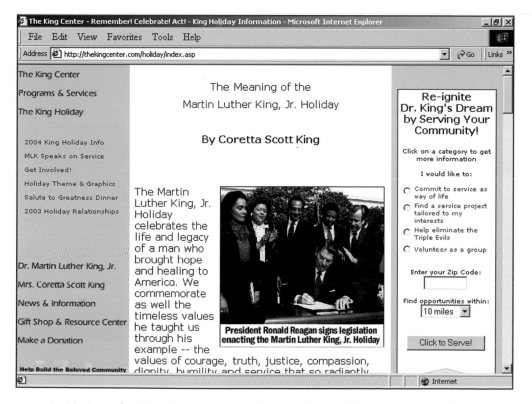

Martin Luther King Day was enacted by President Ronald Reagan in November 1983, but was not first observed until 1986. This national holiday is celebrated on the third Monday in January of each year.

Southern governments still made the process of voting very complicated. They enforced segregation; the practice of keeping white and African-American people separated.

In the mid-1950s, African-American communities were beginning to challenge segregation. In some states, though, racial segregation was the law. These were called "Jim Crow" laws. Those who protested against these laws were often met with violence such as a bomb exploding on their front porch—or worse.

▶ We Want to Love Our Enemies

The night Martin Luther King, Jr.'s, house was bombed, white policemen rushed to the scene. Even the Montgomery mayor came to see what was happening. The policemen and mayor found themselves facing a furious African-American crowd.

King stood on his shattered front porch and said to the crowd, "Please be peaceful."[4] He reminded them, "We believe in law and order." The twenty-seven-year-old minister asked the people not to panic. He advised them not to get weapons. He wanted no violence.

"We want to love our enemies," King said. "I want you to love our enemies. Be good to them. Love them and let them know you love them."[5]

The scene could have easily become deadly. Instead, King's words helped turn both the angry crowd and the policemen away from violence.

Many people were amazed at this young minister. How could he stand on his shattered front porch and ask his friends not to strike back? Where had this man come from? What inspired him to behave this way?

▶ King's Home in Atlanta

The Martin Luther King, Jr., National Historic Site in Atlanta, Georgia, helps find answers to such questions. King was born in

File Edit View Favorites Tools Help

Address http://www.nps.gov/malu/graphics/VC_TULIPS.jpg

MARTIN LUTHER KING, JR. NATIONAL HISTORIC SITE

Done Internet

The Martin Luther King, Jr., National Historic Site is located on Auburn Avenue. In front of the center is the Peace Plaza, which contains an International World Peace Rose Garden and the "BEHOLD" statue.

Atlanta in 1929. He grew up in a segregated neighborhood near the downtown area.

In his home, his church, and his community, Martin Luther King, Jr., learned about his world. He heard family, neighbors, and pastors discuss how society could be better for African Americans. King came to believe that things could be changed without attacking other people.

The Martin Luther King, Jr., National Historic Site and Preservation District was created on October 10, 1980. It was established by an act of Congress that was signed by President Jimmy Carter. The site protects and interprets the places where Dr. King was born, grew up, and is buried.

In the Atlanta Neighborhood

"Atlanta is home for me," Martin Luther King, Jr., said. He called the neighborhood where he grew up a "wholesome community." He added that, "crime was at a minimum, and most of our neighbors were deeply religious."[1]

King's childhood neighborhood centered around Auburn Avenue. Between 1910 and 1930, this was an area of successful

http://www.nps.gov/malu/graphics/birth_home_block.jpg - Microsoft Internet Explorer

File   Edit   View   Favorites   Tools   Help

Address   http://www.nps.gov/malu/graphics/birth_home_block.jpg   Go

Done   Internet

▲ *The Sweet Auburn section of Atlanta, Georgia, was called "The Richest Negro Street in the World" by* Fortune *magazine in 1956. Martin Luther King, Jr., grew up on this block in Sweet Auburn.*

African-American businesses. The churches were well attended. The residents lived in well-kept homes.

Though no one in the Auburn Avenue neighborhood was wealthy, life there was comfortable. The area was seen as a symbol of success in a world that was difficult for African Americans. So the neighborhood came to be called "Sweet Auburn."[2]

The Great Depression was hard on the entire country. It also took a toll on the Sweet Auburn community. Some African-American professionals moved out of the area. Some residents who stayed could not keep up their property as well as they had in the past. The neighborhood began to show signs of poverty and neglect. Even so, it was still a pleasant place to live when King was a youngster. The neighborhood began to recover throughout the 1940s and 1950s.

A Variety of People

Housing in Atlanta was segregated. That meant African Americans could live only in certain parts of the city. So middle-class and poorer African-American families usually lived in the same area.[3]

In Sweet Auburn, African-American teachers and other professionals—ministers, skilled craftsmen, laborers, and domestic workers—were all part of the community. African-American business owners operated food and drug stores, movie theaters, barber shops, beauty parlors, banks, insurance companies, restaurants, newspapers, and meeting halls.

The churches in Sweet Auburn were centers of spiritual and social life.[4] "Daddy" King was pastor of the most well-known church in Sweet Auburn. There were also women's clubs, an orphanage, a school, social clubs, libraries, and a YMCA. Community organizations encouraged their members to help themselves and each other.

Sweet Auburn Today

Auburn Avenue is at the heart of the Martin Luther King, Jr., National Historic Site. There, and on nearby streets, the National

▲ *Visitor Arlene Jackson studies the exhibit containing Martin Luther King, Jr.'s, death certificates. Meanwhile, in the background, other visitors are reading about life on Auburn Avenue.*

Historic Site has recreated the appearance of King's boyhood neighborhood. Some of the buildings are managed in partnership with the National Park Service.

A larger Preservation District surrounds the National Historic Site. This community includes preserved and restored churches, community buildings, music clubs, restaurants, and markets. To preserve something means to protect it from damage and decay. To restore it means to bring it back to an earlier, better condition.

Recently-built homes in the Preservation District have been designed to fit in well with older styles. Museums and libraries provide information on African-American history.

On the grounds of the National Historic Site, the house where King was born is open to the public. The church where he was a member and later a pastor is also open. The community fire station is now a museum.

Houses in the Historic Center

Families in Sweet Auburn lived in one- and two-story homes with inviting front porches. Some of the simpler residences in this area are called "shotgun houses." These are one room wide, and several rooms deep. Each room opens directly into the next, and the connecting doors are lined up.

Imagine someone firing a shotgun through the front door when all the doors were open. The shot could pass out the back door without hitting anything in between. That is where the name "shotgun house" comes from.

Fire Station No. 6, part of the Martin Luther King, Jr., National Historic Site, sits on the corner of Auburn Avenue and Boulevard. The fire station served the Sweet Auburn community from 1894 until 1991.

There are also many double shotgun houses—two shotgun houses joined with a common wall. These share a front porch, and a separate front door opens into each house.

The National Park Service has bought a row of shotgun houses on Auburn Avenue. They are restoring these houses to look like they did in the 1930s. The restored houses have modern interiors, and they are rented out. Unlike the house where King was born, these are private residences and not open to the public.

The Neighborhood Fire Station

Around the corner from the restored houses, Fire Station No. 6 is on a street called Boulevard. The red brick building was built in 1894. It features arched fire engine doors and windows, and decorative brickwork. Fire Station No. 6 is the oldest of Atlanta's early firehouses still in existence. The building has been restored to look as it did when King grew up in the neighborhood.

Now the fire station is a museum, with exhibits of historical fire-fighting equipment. A 1927 American LaFrance fire engine is on display.[5] At the fire station, visitors can learn about the integration of Atlanta's fire department in 1963.

The building also houses the Eastern National Bookstore, which carries books, posters, and other materials related to King, the civil rights movement, and African-American history. Monies from the bookstore go to the National Park Service.[6]

The King Center

Across Boulevard from the fire station is the Martin Luther King, Jr., Center for Nonviolent Social Change. It is often simply called the King Center, for short. The center was founded by King's widow, Coretta Scott King, in 1968. It is designed as a memorial to King and his work. Its buildings and gardens occupy an entire city block.[7]

The King Center exhibits information about King and his work. It also reaches out to educate people worldwide about his

▲ *Dr. Martin Luther King, Jr.'s, tomb made of white Georgia marble rests in part of the Freedom Plaza at the King Center. Inscribed on the tomb is one of the most famous quotes of the civil rights movement.*

nonviolent methods of resolving conflicts. It continues to promote his efforts.[8] The Visitor Center at Freedom Hall in the King Center is open daily.

Martin Luther King, Jr.'s, tomb is at the King Center. It is located in Freedom Plaza, at one end of a reflecting pool.

▷ Major Attractions in the Neighborhood

Martin Luther King, Jr., lived his first twelve years in this Atlanta neighborhood. Here he first faced prejudice and segregation. Here he also learned about family and love.

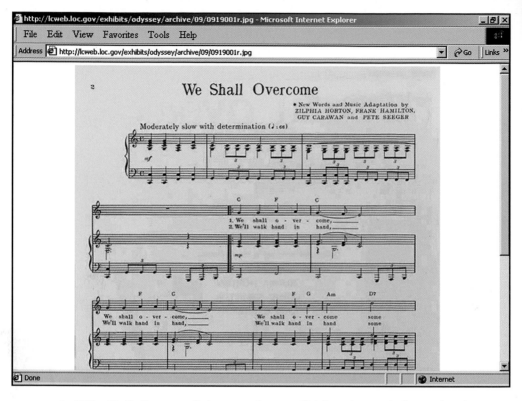

▲ "We Shall Overcome" became the unofficial anthem of the civil rights movement of the 1960s. It was first sung in 1945 by striking tobacco workers in Charleston, South Carolina.

Across Boulevard from the King Center is Ebenezer Baptist Church. As a child, King went to church there. As an adult, he was co-pastor with his father. The house where King was born is on Auburn Avenue, near the restored shotgun houses. These places look much as they did when King was a boy growing up in the neighborhood.

The Family Home

About noon on January 15, 1929, Martin Luther King, Jr., was born in the Sweet Auburn section of Atlanta. The attractive two-story house at 501 Auburn Avenue was built in 1895.[1] King's maternal grandparents had bought the house for $3,500.00 in 1909. Young King lived there with his parents and other relatives until he was twelve. After that, the family moved a few blocks away to a house on Boulevard.

▲ Michael Luther King, Jr., was born on January 15, 1929, in this house on Auburn Street in Atlanta, Georgia. When he was five years old, his father changed both his own name and his son's name to Martin.

The house has decorative woodwork on the porch and an oval window next to the front door. The wide front porch wraps around the side of the building.[2] Now more than one hundred years old, the Birth Home has been restored for visitors to enjoy.

Because of the house's size, there are limits on the number of people who can tour at one time. The Park Service recommends buying tickets for a tour early in the day.[3]

Each December, King's home is decorated as it would have been during Christmas holidays in the 1930s. On certain days, the Birth Home is opened for candlelight tours.[4]

Inside the Birth Home

Inside, the home looks much as it did when young King lived there. The walls are papered in traditional patterns. Polished woodwork and wood furniture give the rooms a warm glow. The furnishings are simple and comfortable.

The front door of the King family home opens into a wide hallway. The family entertained guests in the first room on the left—the parlor, or formal living room. Meetings concerning the church or civil rights activities were held in the parlor. Sometimes the church choir rehearsed there.[5]

The study is a little farther down the hall on the left. This was the place for family games and listening to the radio.[6] Beyond the study is the dining room, where the King family sat down to dinner together every night. This is where the family talked about the events of the day at school, at church, and in the neighborhood. The children were also encouraged to discuss things happening in the nation and around the world.[7]

The first floor also includes a bedroom, kitchen, and laundry. The other bedrooms are upstairs, where King and his brother shared a room. Their sister described the boys' bedroom as always in "great disarray," scattered with clothes, toys, and books. And that is exactly how visitors see the boys' room today.[8]

The King Family

King's parents were the Reverend Martin Luther King, Sr., and Alberta Williams King. Their first child was a girl, Christine. Martin Luther King, Jr., was the second, and the third was Alfred Daniel King. Since he was named after his father, Martin Luther King, Jr., was called "M. L." in his early days.[9]

In his autobiography, King describes his mother, also called "Mama King" or "Mother Dear," as "a devout person . . . soft-spoken and easy-going." He also describes her struggles to explain discrimination and segregation to a small child. She taught him about slavery, the Civil War, and the racial problems that continued into their own time.

President Lyndon B. Johnson (seated at table) signed the Civil Rights Act of 1964 on July 2, 1964. This was followed a year later by a stronger and more effective law called the Voting Rights Act of 1965.

"She taught me that I should feel a sense of 'somebodiness,'" King wrote. "But that on the other hand I had to go out and face a system that stared me in the face every day saying you are 'less than,' you are 'not equal to.'"[10]

M. L.'s father was a strong and forceful man who stood up for his rights. Dr. King—often called "Daddy" King—was the pastor of Ebenezer Baptist Church in Sweet Auburn.[11]

Though his family was not rich, M. L. always had the basic necessities of life. He also felt that he could turn to his father when he had problems.[12]

Jim Crow Laws

Many people called the laws that enforced segregation "Jim Crow" laws. The name probably came from a character in nineteenth-century minstrel shows (stage performances by white actors in black makeup).[13] In a majority of Southern states, Jim Crow laws made it illegal for members of races to mix.

That meant that white and African-American citizens had to be kept separate in many locations. Although Jim Crow laws varied from state to state, many public places were segregated. These included businesses; trains and buses; including waiting rooms and ticket windows; restaurants and lunch counters; public restrooms; water fountains; hospital wards; public parks, beaches, and swimming pools; sports; schools; libraries; and telephone booths. People of different races were forbidden to get married, and if they lived together without marriage, they could be fined or jailed.[14]

M. L. learned about Jim Crow laws at an early age. As he grew up, M. L. also became aware of how "Daddy" King and others in the neighborhood resisted such treatment. Both M. L.'s father and grandfather worked to register African-American voters. They fought for, and won, the creation of a high school for African Americans in Atlanta. "Daddy" King was an active member of the National Association for the Advancement of Colored People (NAACP).[15]

▲ *Martin Luther King, Jr., sits at a press conference in 1966. Ever since the reverend was a child, he knew that he wanted to serve mankind.*

▶ Facing Prejudice

While M. L. was still small, he went to a shoe store with his father. As was the rule, the white clerk politely asked them to take seats in the back of the store. M. L.'s father, though, refused to sit in the back. "Daddy" King took his son by the hand and walked out of the store.[16]

http://lcweb.loc.gov/exhibits/odyssey/archive/09/0909001r.jpg - Microsoft Internet Explorer

File   Edit   View   Favorites   Tools   Help

Address http://lcweb.loc.gov/exhibits/odyssey/archive/09/0909001r.jpg   Go   Links »

Done   Internet

▲ *Three students from North Carolina Agricultural and Technical College are shown here sitting at the lunch counter of an F.W. Woolworth store in Greensboro, North Carolina, in 1960. This was the beginning of many student sit-ins.*

Young M. L. had a white playmate whose father owned a store in the community. When the boys were six years old, things changed. They were sent to separate, segregated schools. Soon afterward, M. L.'s friend told him that they could not play together anymore.[17]

"For a long, long time I could not go swimming," King later wrote, "until there was a Negro YMCA. A Negro child in Atlanta could not go to any public park. I could not go to the so-called white schools. In many of the stores downtown, I couldn't go to a lunch counter to buy a hamburger or a cup of coffee. I could not attend any of the theaters."[18]

When he was fourteen, King traveled to another town to participate in a speaking contest. His speech on "The Negro and the Constitution" won the competition.

In his speech, King said that a true democracy could not keep one group of people living in ignorance. "We cannot be truly Christian people so long as we flout the central teachings of Jesus: brotherly love and the Golden Rule." He added that "if freedom is good for any, it is good for all."[19]

That night, King and his teacher returned to Atlanta by bus. When some white passengers boarded, the driver ordered King and his teacher to get up and give their seats to the white passengers. "We didn't move quickly enough to suit him, so he began cursing us." The teacher urged young King to obey the law. The two of them rode standing up for the whole 90-mile trip. King later wrote that he had never before been so angry.[20]

When he was fifteen, King graduated from his high school to Atlanta's Morehouse College. While he was a student at Morehouse, he took part in peaceful student sit-ins at segregated lunch counters in the city.

During his early years, the greatest question in King's mind came to be, "How could I love a race of people who hated me . . . ?"[21]

Back	Forward	Stop	Review	Home	Explore	Favorites	History

Chapter 4 ▶

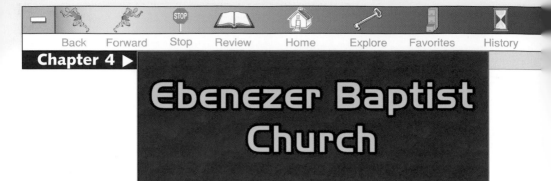

Ebenezer Baptist Church

On Auburn Avenue, two blocks from Martin Luther King, Jr.'s, boyhood home, is Ebenezer Baptist Church. It is a red brick building with sturdy towers standing on each side of the main entrance. The church was founded in 1886, and the current building was completed in 1922. Ebenezer Baptist is managed and operated by the National Park Service and is open to the public.[1]

Ebenezer Baptist Church is still very much as it appeared from 1929 until 1941. Inside, polished wooden pews gleam in a

▲ *Martin Luther King, Jr., his father, and his grandfather all served as pastor of Ebenezer Baptist Church.*

△ *In the spring of 1948, Martin Luther King, Jr., (circled) graduated from Morehouse College with a Bachelor of Arts degree in sociology.*

white sanctuary. Colored light from stained glass windows falls across the room.[2]

M. L. began attending church services at age five. He later wrote that "the church has always been a second home for me. As far back as I can remember, I was in church every Sunday. My best friends were in Sunday school, and it was the Sunday school that helped me to build the capacity for getting along with people."[3]

▶ The Church and the Community

Clergymen have always played strong roles in African-American communities. They have been respected and looked upon as authorities. They have worked to improve the lives of their congregations.

The pastors of Ebenezer Baptist Church supported the development of local black businesses. These pastors urged a way of life based on Christian beliefs—stressing love, equality, and nonviolence.

When M. L. was growing up, "Daddy" King was pastor of Ebenezer Baptist Church. At age eighteen, M. L. himself gave a trial sermon to the congregation. Soon afterward, M. L. was ordained a minister.

The young Dr. King, Jr., earned his Bachelor of Divinity degree from Crozer Theological Seminary in 1951. He earned his doctorate degree in philosophy from Boston University in 1955.

▶ Thoreau and Gandhi

Martin Luther King, Jr.'s, policy of nonviolence grew out of his strong religious background. During his college and seminary studies, he learned about others who taught nonviolence. Henry David Thoreau (1817–62) and Mohandas Gandhi (1869–1948) both believed that society could be changed without using violence.

Thoreau was an American author who wrote about nature and about the human spirit. In 1849, he spent a night in jail. He had refused to pay a tax that supported the Mexican-American War. Thoreau considered the war immoral. He believed that it was mainly an effort to gain more land where slavery could be practiced.

Thoreau believed that society could be changed through peaceful civil disobedience. That meant refusing to obey a law that he believed to be unjust. In his essay "Civil Disobedience," Thoreau said, "It is not desirable to cultivate a respect for the law, so much as for the right. The only obligation which I have a right to assume is to do at any time what I think right."[4]

Mohandas Gandhi was a British-educated Indian lawyer. He had read the writings of Thoreau and others on civil disobedience. Gandhi organized protests against British rule in India and South Africa. Gandhi and his followers were sometimes jailed for their nonviolent resistance to unjust laws, but their protests helped gain independence for the country of India.

In 1948, Gandhi was assassinated. He was shot by a fanatic who hated his message of tolerance for all beliefs.[5] Gandhi

▲ *Booker T. Washington (upper left) and Mohandas K. Gandhi (upper right) were great inspirations to Martin Luther King, Jr. Gandhi especially, inspired King to use civil disobedience in his fight for civil rights.*

became a model for many African Americans who wanted to change society. The King Center includes exhibits about Gandhi and his work.[6]

Young Martin Luther King studied the words and deeds of Thoreau and Gandhi at Crozer. In 1959, King traveled to India and met with some of Gandhi's followers. King became convinced that nonviolent civil disobedience was the best way to change things in his own country.[7]

▶ Practicing Nonviolence

Martin Luther King began practicing nonviolence when he returned from India. The peaceful student sit-ins at segregated lunch counters in 1960 helped to open Atlanta's public restaurants and other public services to all races.

King's beliefs were severely tested in Montgomery, Alabama. He was elected president of the Montgomery Improvement Association during the bus boycott. King remembered what he had learned at home, at church, in his neighborhood, and from his studies.

King insisted that the MIA's protests be nonviolent. Those who joined the boycott were taught how to respond to attacks—both verbal and physical—without striking back.[8]

King would later teach and demonstrate nonviolence in other states and in many difficult situations during the civil rights movement.

▲ The Civil Rights Memorial, located in Montgomery, Alabama, contains a circular fountain with a time line of important events in the civil rights movement. It begins with the 1954 Brown vs. the Board of Education decision and ends with Martin Luther King, Jr.'s, death in 1968.

▶ Returning to Ebenezer Baptist

In 1956, an education building was added to Ebenezer Baptist Church. That building soon became the center for meetings where people discussed the problems of African-American inequality and segregation.

In 1957, the Southern Christian Leadership Conference (SCLC) was founded at Ebenezer Baptist. Martin Luther King, Jr., became the organization's first president. African-American church groups across the South joined the SCLC. The organization played a powerful role in ending segregation and gaining the right to vote for African Americans.[9]

In 1960, Martin Luther King, Jr., moved his family from Montgomery back to Atlanta. He became a co-pastor of Ebenezer Baptist Church with his father. By that time, the pastors of African-American churches were leading the long struggle against inequality and segregation.

The membership of Ebenezer Baptist included African-American lawyers, teachers, and other professionals as well as everyday working people and family members of all ages. They were all segregated from the white community. They all suffered from inequality in schools and other public services. Churches such as Ebenezer Baptist brought together large numbers of people who took action against segregation.[10]

Martin Luther King, Jr., remained co-pastor of Ebenezer Baptist Church until his death at the hand of an assassin. His funeral was held there on April 9, 1968.

His father, the Reverend Martin Luther King, Sr., retired from the ministry on August 1, 1975.[11] In 1999, the new Horizon Sanctuary was opened across the street from Ebenezer Baptist Church. Horizon is home to the present-day congregation.[12]

Where Did It All Lead?

The Southern Christian Leadership Conference, which King helped found, has its headquarters in Atlanta. King served as SCLC president and board member. King also joined lunch counter boycotts and supported a union strike in Atlanta. However, most of his best-known civil rights activities took place outside of Atlanta.[1]

▶ Civil Rights

The legal rights of a nation's people are called "civil rights." In America, these include freedom of speech, press, and assembly; the

▲ *Martin Luther King, Jr.'s, tomb is located in the middle of the reflecting pool at the King Center in Atlanta, Georgia.*

A crowd of approximately 250,000 people demonstrated in front of the steps of the Lincoln Memorial during the March on Washington, D.C., on August 28, 1963. Martin Luther King, Jr., waves to the crowd before his famous "I Have a Dream" speech.

right to vote; freedom from involuntary servitude (slavery); and the right to equal treatment in public places and equal protection under the law for all Americans. The drive toward equal rights for African Americans was called the civil rights movement. Many historians say that the civil rights movement started with the bus boycott in Montgomery, Alabama.

Martin Luther King, Jr., was one of the great leaders of America's civil rights movement. He always taught that efforts to achieve equality must be nonviolent. King was put in jail on several occasions for his activities. Along with others who struggled for freedom, he often faced violence and great danger. Still, he stuck by his beliefs and his goals.

Marches and Speeches

During the 1960s, African Americans made many efforts to gain their rights as citizens. Working with the SCLC and other organizations, King organized huge peaceful marches and demonstrations.

After a march in Birmingham, Alabama, King and others were arrested and jailed. In his famous "Letter From Birmingham Jail," King answered criticism from other clergymen. They had called his actions extreme. King commented, "Oppressed people cannot remain oppressed forever. The yearning for freedom eventually manifests itself . . ."[2]

During the civil rights movement, King's public speeches moved countless people. Perhaps his most famous speech was given on August 28, 1963, in Washington, D.C., King stood on the steps of the Lincoln Memorial. About 250,000 people filled the area in front of him all the way to the Washington Monument.

"I have a dream," said King. And he spoke of all the things that he dreamed. He hoped the nation would live up to its belief that all are created equal. He spoke of peace, brotherhood, freedom, and justice. He ended his speech with the words, "Free at last, free at last. Thank God Almighty, we are free at last."[3]

▶ The Nobel Peace Prize

In 1964, Martin Luther King, Jr., was honored with the Nobel Peace Prize. At thirty-five, he was the youngest man ever to receive the prize. He was the second American to be awarded this Nobel.[4]

King traveled to Oslo, Norway, to accept the award and to give his Nobel lecture. He spoke of "modern man's scientific and technological progress" but added that "something basic is missing." King continued,

> There is a sort of poverty of the spirit which stands in glaring contrast to our scientific and technological abundance. The richer we have become materially, the poorer we have become morally and spiritually. We have learned to fly the air like birds and swim the sea like fish, but we have not learned the simple art of living together as brothers.[5]

▲ *Martin Luther King, Jr., was named Man of the Year by* Time *magazine in 1964. He won the Nobel Peace Prize the same year.*

▶ Assassination

The American who did most to change society by nonviolent means was killed by an act of violence. On April 4, 1968, Martin Luther King, Jr., was standing on his motel balcony in Memphis, Tennessee. He had come to Memphis to speak for the city's garbage workers, who were on strike.

A shot rang out. King was struck in the neck by a bullet. He was rushed to a hospital, but died less than an hour later. King was just thirty-nine when he was killed. James Earl Ray was arrested for the murder. He confessed, was convicted, and was jailed. Ray later recanted his confession, but he died in jail in 1998.

▲ *This image shows the window from which James Earl Ray is said to have fired the fatal shot that killed Martin Luther King, Jr. The building in the background was the Lorraine Motel, but is now the National Civil Rights Museum in Memphis, Tennessee.*

Much of the nation, black and white, was horrified over King's assassination. African Americans demonstrated in more than 125 cities. Some of the demonstrations turned into violent riots. America was also shaken by other assassinations during that decade such as the deaths of President John F. Kennedy and his brother, former Attorney General Robert Kennedy.

Robert Kennedy was running for president and had made a speech about King. Kennedy said that King had "dedicated his life to love and to justice for his fellow human beings, and he died because of that effort."[6] Robert Kennedy, himself, was shot and killed on June 6, 1968.

▶ Researching Sweet Auburn

A lot of research went into creating the Martin Luther King, Jr., National Historic Site. The National Park Service staff studied the historical background of the area. A team examined neighborhood buildings and written records. They studied maps and materials from many sources.

Researchers put together all the material they could find on the Sweet Auburn neighborhood, the American civil rights movement, and King's life. Then they set about restoring the neighborhood for visitors to enjoy.

▶ Visiting the National Historic Site

The National Park Service Visitor Center is on Auburn Avenue, across the street from Ebenezer Baptist Church and the King Center. Between Auburn Avenue and the Visitor Center is Peace Plaza. The beautifully landscaped plaza includes the Peace Rose Garden and waterfalls.[7]

▲ The National Park Service Visitor Center is on Auburn Avenue. The Visitor Center features exhibits about Dr. King's life and the civil rights movement.

The eternal flame, located in front of Martin Luther King, Jr.'s, tomb at the King Center, symbolizes the continuing fight for equality and harmony among the races.

An information desk at the Visitor Center helps visitors with maps, tickets, and questions. The center also features a "Children of Courage" exhibit, showing how children participated in the civil rights movement. The Visitor Center's "Courage To Lead" exhibit focuses on Martin Luther King, Jr.'s, life and activities. A selection of Jim Crow laws are posted at these exhibits.

The Visitor Center holds a concert series and a film series. The theater shows videos about the people of the civil rights movement.[8] The National Historic Site also sponsors special events. These include a celebration of King's birthday on January 15, Martin Luther King Day (third Monday of January), Black History Month each February, and a remembrance of King's assassination each April.[9]

On the other side of the Visitor Center is the King-Carter Freedom Peace Walk. The walk links the Martin Luther King, Jr., National Historic Site with the Carter Presidential Center and Library.

A visit to the Martin Luther King, Jr., National Historic Site informs visitors about Martin Luther King, Jr., and the civil rights movement. It brings King's early neighborhood to life, and it helps find some answers to often-asked questions—such as how a young preacher could stand on his bombed porch and insist that we must love our enemies.

Glossary

boycott—An organized refusal to buy goods or services from a person, business, or organization in order to force policy changes through economic and social pressure.

Civil Rights Act of 1964—Legislation signed on July 2, 1964, by President Lyndon B. Johnson, banning segregation in facilities offering public services and outlawing discrimination in hiring.

civil rights movement—Movement beginning in the 1960s to establish civil rights for African-American citizens.

congregation—A group of people of the same denomination that meet for worship and religious instruction.

Fifteenth Amendment—An amendment to the U.S. Constitution ratified on February 3, 1870, guaranteeing every American citizen the right to vote regardless of race, color, or previous enslavement.

Fourteenth Amendment—An amendment to the U.S. Constitution adopted on July 28, 1868, protecting every American citizen from state laws that attempt to deprive people of their rights listed in the Bill of Rights.

Jim Crow laws—Laws passed enforcing segregation and discrimination against African Americans.

poll tax—A tax levied on the right to vote. These taxes were usually put into effect to stop poor African Americans from voting.

seamstress—A woman who makes her living by sewing.

segregation—The separation or isolation of groups of peoples based on race, class, or ethnic group.

Southern Christian Leadership Conference (SCLC)—African-American church organization founded in 1957 by Reverand Martin Luther King, Jr., that played an important role in the fight to end segregation and give African Americans the right to vote.

Sweet Auburn—An area of Atlanta, Georgia, that extends for 1.5 miles along Auburn Avenue. At one time it was considered to be the wealthiest African-American street in the United States.

Voting Rights Act—Legislation signed on August 6, 1965, by President Lyndon B. Johnson, outlawing the requirement of literacy in order to vote.

Chapter 1. "Please Be Peaceful"

1. Martin Luther King, Jr., *The Autobiography of Martin Luther King, Jr.*, Clayborne Carson, ed. (New York: Warner Books, 1998), p. 78.

2. Ibid., p. 79.

3. Ibid.

4. Staff, *I Have a Dream: the Story of Martin Luther King in Text and Pictures* (New York: Time-Life Books, 1968), p. 10.

5. King, p. 80.

Chapter 2. In the Atlanta Neighborhood

1. Martin Luther King, Jr., *The Autobiography of Martin Luther King, Jr.*, Clayborne Carson, ed. (New York: Warner Books, 1998), p. 2.

2. National Park Service, "Sweet Auburn Historic District," Atlanta, n.d., <http://www.cr.nps.gov/nr/travel/atlanta/aub.htm> (June 29, 2004).

3. Robert W. Blythe, Maureen A. Carroll, and Steven H. Moffson, "The Development of a Black Community and Leader," *Martin Luther King, Jr., Historic Resource Study,* August 1994, <http://www.nps.gov/malu/hrs/HRS1.HTM> (February 12, 2004).

4. Ibid.

5. "The Development of a Black Community and Leader," (February 12, 2004).

6. Interpretive Staff, "Eastern National Bookstore," *Martin Luther King, Jr., National Historic Site,* November 12, 2003, <http://www.nps.gov/malu/documents/eastern_national_welcome.htm> (February 23, 2004).

7. Interpretive Staff, "The King Center," *Martin Luther King, Jr., National Historic Site,* February 7, 1999, <http://www.nps.gov/malu/documents/kcpage.htm> (February 24, 2004).

8. Ibid.

Chapter 3. The Family Home

1. Robert W. Blythe, Maureen A. Carroll, and Steven H. Moffson, "The Development of a Black Community and Leader," *Martin Luther King, Jr., Historic Resource Study,* August 1994, <http://www.nps.gov/malu/hrs/HRS1.HTM> (February 12, 2004).

2. "Front Porch," *Martin Luther King, Jr., Birth Home Virtual Tour,* n.d., <http://www.nps.gov/malu/BirthHomeTour/mlk_frontporch.html> (February 23, 2004).

3. "Martin Luther King, Jr., National Historic Site: Georgia," National Park Service, n.d., <http://www.nps.gov/malu/> (February 12, 2004).

4. "Annual Events at the National Historic Site," *Martin Luther King, Jr., National Historic Site,* 2004, <http://www.nps.gov/malu/documents/events.htm> (February 18, 2004).

5. "Entrance Hall & The Parlor," *Martin Luther King, Jr., Birth Home Virtual Tour,* n.d., <http://www.nps.gov/malu/BirthHomeTour/mlk_entrance.html> (February 23, 2004).

6. "The Study," *Martin Luther King, Jr., Birth Home Virtual Tour,* n.d., <http://www.nps.gov/malu/BirthHomeTour/mlk_study.html> (February 23, 2004).

7. "Dining Room," *Martin Luther King, Jr., Birth Home Virtual Tour,* n.d., <http://www.nps.gov/malu/BirthHomeTour/mlk_dining.html> (May 21, 2004).

8. "Martin and Alfred's Room," *Martin Luther King, Jr., Birth Home Virtual Tour,* n.d., <http://www.nps.gov/malu/BirthHomeTour/mlk_boysrm.html> (May 21, 2004).

9. "Martin Luther King, Jr., National Historic Site: Georgia," (February 12, 2004).

10. Martin Luther King, Jr., *The Autobiography of Martin Luther King, Jr.,* Clayborne Carson, ed. (New York: Warner Books, 1998), p. 3.

11. Interpretive Staff, "Ebenezer Baptist Church: Heritage Sanctuary," *Martin Luther, King, Jr., National Historic Site,* August 26, 2003, <http://www.nps.gov/malu/documents/ebenezer_church_welcome.htm> (February 12, 2004).

12. King, p. 5.

13. Robert W. Blythe, Maureen A. Carroll, and Steven H. Moffson, "The Development of a Black Community and Leader," *Martin Luther King, Jr., Historic Resource Study,* August 1994, <http://www.nps.gov/malu/hrs/HRS1.HTM> (February 12, 2004).

14. Interpretive Staff, "'Jim Crow' Laws," *Martin Luther King, Jr., National Historic Site,* <http://www.nps.gov/malu/documents/jim_crow_laws.htm> (February 23, 2004).

15. Blythe, Carroll, and Moffson, (February 12, 2004).

16. King, p. 8.

17. Ibid., p. 7.

18. Ibid., p. 8.

19. Ibid., pp. 9–10.

20. Ibid., p. 10.

21. Ibid., p. 7.

Chapter 4. Ebenezer Baptist Church

1. "Martin Luther King, Jr., National Historic Site: Georgia," *National Park Service,* n.d., <http://www.nps.gov/malu/> (February 12, 2004).

2. Rev. Dr. Joseph L. Roberts, "The Heritage Sanctuary," *Historic Ebenezer Baptist Church,* <http://www.historicebenezer.org/HeritageSanctuary.htm> (February 20, 2004).

3. Martin Luther King, Jr., *The Autobiography of Martin Luther King, Jr.,* Clayborne Carson, ed. (New York: Warner Books, 1998), p. 6.

4. Henry David Thoreau, "Resistance to Civil Government, or Civil Disobedience," Webtext created 1999, <http://www.vcu.edu/engweb/transcendentalism/authors/thoreau/civil/> (February 12, 2004).

5. Robin Chew, "Mahatma Gandhi, Indian Spiritual/Political Leader and Humanitarian," 1995–2004, <http://www.lucidcafe.com/library/95oct/mkgandhi.html> (February 12, 2004).

6. "Facilities," *Martin Luther King, Jr., National Historic Site,* n.d., <http://www.nps.gov/malu/documents/facilities.htm> (February 12, 2004).

7. Robin Chew, "Martin Luther King, Jr., Civil-Rights Leader," 1995–2004, <http://www.lucidcafe.com/library/96jan/king.html> (February 14, 2004).

8. Robert W. Blythe, Maureen A. Carroll, and Steven H. Moffson, "The Development of a Black Community and Leader," *Martin Luther King, Jr., Historic Resource Study,* August 1994, <http://www.nps.gov/malu/hrs/HRS1.HTM> (February 12, 2004).

9. Ibid.

10. Ibid.

11. Interpretive Staff, "Ebenezer Baptist Church," *Martin Luther King, Jr., National Historic Site,* January 5, 1998, <http://www.nps.gov/malu/documents/ebcpage.htm> (February 12, 2004).

12. Interpretive Staff, "Ebenezer Baptist Church History," *Martin Luther King, Jr., National Historic Site,* January 5, 1998, <http://www.nps.gov/malu/documents/ebenezer_church_history.htm> (February 12, 2004).

Chapter 5. Where Did It All Lead?

1. Robert W. Blythe, Maureen A. Carroll, and Steven H. Moffson, "The Development of a Black Community and Leader," *Martin Luther King, Jr., Historic Resource Study,* August 1994, <http://www.nps.gov/malu/hrs/HRS1.HTM> (February 12, 2004).

2. Dr. Martin Luther King, Jr., "Letter from Birmingham Jail," *Frequently Requested Documents,* April 16, 1963, <http://www.stanford.edu/group/King/popular_requests/frequentdocs/birmingham.pdf> (February 25, 2004).

3. Dr. Martin Luther King, Jr., "I Have a Dream," *A Call to Conscience: The Landmark Speeches of Dr. Martin Luther King, Jr.,* August 28, 1963, <http://www.stanford.edu/group/King/publications/speeches/address_at_march_on_washington.pdf> (February 25, 2004).

4. "Biographical Outline of Dr. Martin Luther King, Jr.," *The King Center,* n.d., <http://thekingcenter.com/mlk/bio.html> (February 12, 2004).

5. Frederick W. Haberman, "Martin Luther King—Nobel Lecture," *The Nobel Foundation,* December 11, 1964, <http://www.nobel.se/peace/laureates/1964/king-lecture.html> (February 25, 2004).

6. Robert Kennedy, "Statement on the Assassination of Martin Luther King, Jr.," *John Fitzgerald Kennedy Library,* April 4, 1968, <http://www/.cs.umb.edu/jfklibrary/r040468.htm> (June 7, 2004).

7. Interpretive Staff, "Peace Plaza," *Martin Luther King, Jr., National Historic Site,* February 27, 2003, <http://www.nps.gov/malu/documents/plaza_welcome.htm> (February 25, 2004).

8. Interpretive Staff, "National Park Service Visitor Center," *Martin Luther King, Jr., National Historic Site,* October 8, 2003, <http://www.nps.gov/malu/documents/visitor_center_welcome.htm> (February 18, 2004).

9. "Annual Events at the National Historic Site," *Martin Luther King, Jr., National Historic Site,* 2004, <http://www.nps.gov/malu/documents/events.htm> (February 18, 2004).

Ayers, Alex. *The Wisdom of Martin Luther King, Jr.: An A-Z Guide to the Ideas and Ideals of the Great Civil Rights Leader.* New York: Meridian Books, 1993.

Bray, Rosemary L. *Dreams: The Story of Martin Luther King, Jr.* New York: Greenwillow Books, 1995.

Ching, Jacqueline. *The Assassination of Martin Luther King, Jr.* New York: Rosen Publishing Group, Inc., 2001.

Haskins, Jim. *I Have a Dream: The Life and Words of Martin Luther King, Jr.* Boston: Houghton Mifflin Company, 1992.

King, Martin Luther, Jr. *The Words of Martin Luther King, Jr.* (selected by Coretta Scott King). New York: Newmarket Press, 1983.

McKissack, Patricia, and Fredrick McKissack. *Martin Luther King, Jr.: Man of Peace.* Berkeley Heights, N.J.: Enslow Publishers, Inc., 2001.

Posner, Gerald. *Killing the Dream: James Earl Ray and the Assassination of Martin Luther King, Jr.* New York: Random House, 1998.

Santella, Andrew. *Martin Luther King, Jr.: Civil Rights Leader and Nobel Prize Winner.* Chanhassen, Minn.: Child's World, 2004.

Schuman, Michael A. *Martin Luther King, Jr.: Leader for Civil Rights.* Berkeley Heights, N.J.: Enslow Publishers, Inc., 1996.

Siebold, Thomas. ed. *Martin Luther King, Jr.* Farmington Hills, Mich.: Gale Group, 2000.

Swygert, Dorothy. *The March for Justice: Martin Luther King's Rise to Fame.* Laurelton, N.Y.: Rekindling the Heart Publications, 1997.

Wukovitz, John F. *Martin Luther King, Jr.* San Diego, Calif.: Lucent Books, 1999.

Index